JUSTICE
Makes a Difference

by Dr. Artika Tyner
and Jacklyn Milton

illustrations by
Jeremy Norton
and Janos Orban

W9-CKC-462

★ **The Story of Miss Freedom Fighter, Esquire** ★

Text copyright © 2017 Dr. Artika Tyner and Jacklyn Milton
Illustrations copyright © 2017 Book Bridge Press
Illustrations by Jeremy Norton and Janos Orban
Design by Lois Rainwater
All rights reserved.

No part of this book may be reproduced in any manner
without the express written consent of the publisher,
except in the case of brief excerpts in critical reviews and articles.

All inquiries or sales requests should be addressed to:

Planting People Growing Justice Press
P.O. Box 131894
Saint Paul, MN 55113
www.ppgjli.org

Printed and bound in the United States of America

First Edition
LCCN 2017912940
HC ISBN 978-0-9985553-1-7   SC ISBN 978-0-9985553-0-0
10 9 8 7 6 5 4 3 2 1   10 9 8 7 6 5 4 3 2 1

This book was expertly produced by Book Bridge Press
www.bookbridgepress.com

This book is dedicated

to the loving memory of our grandmothers,

Ruth, Nellie, Rosie, and Nadine,

who taught us

the importance of

love, leadership, and service.

—A. T. *and* J. M.

Justice's favorite place to visit was her grandma's house. Grandma always greeted her with the biggest, warmest hug. Grandma always made Justice feel important.

The best part of Grandma's house was her den full of books. Justice and Grandma would spend hours together in the den, talking and reading.

"Your name is your destiny," Grandma had been telling Justice since the day she was born. Grandma reminded her often that being named Justice came with great responsibility. "To whom much is given, much is accounted for," Grandma always said.

Justice might not have understood all the words that Grandma said, but she understood that she was meant to serve and lead in her community.

One day when Justice was visiting, Grandma asked, "What is in your hands to make a difference in the world?"

What can I do? Justice wondered. *I am only eight years old. How can I make a difference?*

Grandma served in the church. She fed the hungry, sheltered the homeless, clothed those in need, and visited the sick. Grandma described this as living out her faith.

Justice wanted to be like her grandma. She wanted to know how she could live out her faith.

Grandma found Justice in the den, heavy with thought. "Tell me what's bothering you, Justice," Grandma said.

"I want to live out my faith like you, Grandma, but I am only eight years old," Justice said. "What can I do? Aren't I too young?"

Grandma's smile was gentle and reassuring. "Your age does not show what you are capable of, so don't let someone tell you that you're too young to make a difference."

"Justice, do you remember the poem you wrote for the Rev. Dr. Martin Luther King Jr. celebration at your school?" Grandma asked. "That poem made a difference."

Justice remembered the applause of her teachers and classmates. She knew her grandma's words were true.

Grandma gave Justice a book. "Here's a book about someone else who made a difference through her writing."

Justice spent the rest of the afternoon reading about Ida B. Wells.

Ida B. Wells was a journalist who used her writing to advance racial equality. She skillfully wielded her pen to wage war for justice through her work as editor of the *Memphis Free Speech and Headlight*. She continued to advance social change while serving as a journalist with Chicago's *Daily Inter Ocean* and the *Chicago Conservator,* one of the oldest African American newspapers in the United States.

Justice was amazed by how Ida B. Wells used her pen to write for justice.

Justice picked up a pen and said, "I can write for justice."

All that week, Justice worked on a poem about love and peace. When Justice visited the next weekend, she showed her grandma the finished poem.

"Words are powerful," Grandma told Justice. "They can be used in powerful ways to do good or to do harm. That's why it's important to always be careful with your words. You did good, Justice."

Justice smiled. Grandma always made her feel proud.

"Justice, I have another book to share with you," Grandma said and handed Justice a book with a picture of a man on the cover who stood larger than life.

"Words can be powerful, and music can be powerful too," Grandma told her.

Justice read all about Paul Robeson, who sang freedom songs in more than twenty different languages. He was a lawyer, a singer, an actor, and a professional athlete. Justice marveled at how talented Paul Robeson was. He was able to touch people's hearts through the power of song. These songs empowered others to join in the fight for freedom and justice.

Justice had grown up hearing her grandma sing powerful songs like, "We Shall Overcome" and Sam Cooke's

"A Change Is Gonna Come." These were freedom songs. When Grandma sang, Justice could feel it all the way down in her toes.

"Grandma," Justice said, "I want to sing for justice. Will you teach me some songs?"

Grandma began to sing, "This little light of mine. I'm gonna let it shine…"

Justice felt a light inside her spark. "Let it shine, let it shine, let it shine!" she sang.

Sometimes when Justice visited, she helped Grandma in the garden. Justice loved the way the warm earth felt under her feet. She was amazed by how the tiniest seed could become a big vine full of juicy red tomatoes or a tall forest of okra plants. Grandma would sing while they worked, and Justice would hum along. Their music served as the rhythm for their digging and planting.

Planting a garden was hard work, and it gave Justice a lot of time to daydream. She fantasized about what it would be like to travel around the globe.

"What's the most exotic place you've ever traveled to, Grandma?" Justice asked dreamily.

Grandma chuckled. "I haven't been much outside St. Paul, honey," Grandma said, "but I've traveled all over the world through books." This made Justice happy, because she loved to travel through books too.

After they were finished in the garden, Grandma gave Justice a book about a woman in a faraway land.

"Happy traveling!" Grandma said.

Justice read all about the country Kenya and the work of Dr. Wangari Maathai.

Dr. Maathai was a global leader. She organized the Green Belt Movement with the hopes of restoring trees in her home country, Kenya. She sought to restore the beauty of nature and uplift the close-knit community. She began by organizing mothers, daughters, and grandmothers to take action by planting one seedling at a time. More than 51 million trees were planted.

Justice had an idea. "Grandma, can we bring the community together like Dr. Maathai and start a community garden?"

Grandma smiled her proudest smile. "I think that's a wonderful idea. Should we invite others to help?"

"Yes!" Justice said. "We can grow fruits and vegetables. Maybe we can ask our neighbors to help us."

During one visit to her grandma's house, Justice was quieter than usual. She sat on her favorite green chair in Grandma's kitchen drinking lemonade.

Grandma looked concerned. "What's troubling you, princess?"

"My friends at school said women can't be president," Justice said. "But I always thought I might grow up to be president someday."

"Justice, don't ever let anyone tell you that you can't be who you want to be."

She wanted to believe her grandma, but she still wasn't sure.

When Justice got home from Grandma's that afternoon, she found a book in her backpack about Shirley Chisholm. She knew it was from her grandma because her grandma always left books in hidden places as special gifts.

Justice read about Shirley Chisholm, who became the first African American woman to run for president of the United States in 1972. She called herself the candidate of the people because she was determined to fight for the rights of all people.

Justice became very excited. "I can be president one day," she said to herself. Then she stood tall and said with confidence, "I can fight for justice!"

Justice couldn't wait to tell her friends at school about Shirley Chisholm. She told her grandma all about it. "Grandma, now all my friends want to be president!"

"I'm counting on it," Grandma said, smiling. "What else are you learning about in school?" she asked.

"This week we learned about the legal case *Brown versus Board of Education*," Justice told her grandma.

Grandma got a faraway look in her eyes. "I remember attending school in a one-room shack in Alabama," she told Justice. "Dozens of students of all ages gathered in the schoolhouse to learn together. We didn't have much, most days not even paper or pencils, but we had a love of learning."

Justice couldn't imagine going to school in a one-room schoolhouse with kids of all different ages. Justice told Grandma she learned that *Brown versus Board of Education* was a case about ending segregation in schools. "Grandma, we learned that black children were not allowed to attend school with white children."

"Yes, Justice. I remember," Grandma said. "The schools were separate and unequal."

"Grandma, we also learned about the lawyer who worked to end segregation in schools." Justice was proud to know such important information.

"Indeed!" Grandma smiled. "Charles Hamilton Houston. He said lawyers should serve as 'a mouthpiece for the weak and a sentinel guarding against wrong.'"

"That's a funny word!" Justice said. "What does it mean to be a 'mouthpiece'?" she asked.

Grandma explained, "A mouthpiece means that you use your voice to share about the challenges people face in society, like ending hunger or ending homelessness."

"What does 'sentinel' mean?"

"How about you find out for yourself in your dictionary," Grandma said with a wink.

Justice ran to find her dictionary. She paged through until she found "sentinel." *A sentinel is a soldier or guard whose job is to stand and keep watch.*

Wow! Justice thought. *I can be a soldier for justice!*

Finally, Justice was sure. She knew she could make a difference in the world by becoming a lawyer. Her love for superheroes inspired her vision for the future. She had a dream of becoming Miss Freedom Fighter, Esquire—a superhero with a law degree and an Afro!

Now Justice could see herself more clearly. She was determined to use her education in the struggle for justice. She finally understood the meaning of her grandma's words, "To whom much is given, much is accounted for." Justice would live up to her name.

"Justice, are you ready for bed?" asked Grandma. Justice could not believe how fast the time went by. She had remained in the den all day with her books.

As she lay down for bed and finished her bedtime prayer with Grandma, Justice said, "Grandma, I will make a difference by becoming a lawyer and helping those in need." Grandma gave her a reassuring smile and kissed Justice good night.

Justice found a book under her pillow—another special gift from Grandma. Justice began reading about Ella Baker.

Ella Baker helped the young people of the civil rights movement get organized and take a stand for equality and freedom.

Justice fell asleep quietly humming Ella's song:

We who believe in freedom cannot rest...

...We who believe in freedom
cannot rest until it comes

To me young people come first,
they have the courage where we fail
And if I can shed some light
as they carry us through the gale

Struggling myself
don't mean a whole lot

I come to realize
That teaching others to
stand up and fight
is the only way my struggle survives

We who believe in freedom
cannot rest
We who believe in freedom
cannot rest until it comes

What is in your hands to make a difference in the world?

Share the lessons you learned from this book.
Inspire your friends and family to make a difference.

Tutor younger students in your school.
Share what you have learned in math, science, and reading.

Help someone in need.
Volunteer to do chores for elders in your community.

Collect food and volunteer at your local food shelf.
Organize a fund-raiser for your favorite charity.

The Leaders Who Inspired Justice

Ida B. Wells
1862–1931

Photo courtesy of New York Public Library

Ida B. Wells was a brave and fearless activist, journalist, suffragist, and feminist who spoke against racial inequalities, rallied for democratic rights, and crusaded against lynchings.

One of her significant accomplishments, *The Red Record*, was a 100-page pamphlet that explored the history of African Americans and examined the causes and statistics about lynchings in the United States.

Paul Robeson
1898–1976

Photo courtesy of New York Public Library

Paul Robeson was a man of many talents. He was an athlete and a performing artist, and he established a popular screen and singing career. Robeson used his fame to speak out against racial inequalities and became a world activist. In the 1940s, Robeson protested the Cold War and headed an organization that encouraged President Truman to stand behind anti-lynching laws. Robeson's outspoken voice caused him to be blacklisted in the entertainment industry, as well as have his passport revoked in 1950.

Dr. Wangari Maathai

1940–2011

Photo courtesy of Wikimedia Commons

Dr. Wangari Maathai was internationally known as an environmental political activist and a Nobel Peace Prize recipient for her work in founding the Green Belt Movement, an environmental, nongovernmental organization based in Nairobi, Kenya. Established in 1977, the Green Belt Movement organizes women in rural parts of Kenya to plant trees, which replenishes the communities' main source of fuel for cooking, creates income, and stops soil erosion. The movement has planted 51 million trees and more than 30,000 women have been trained in a trade that helps women earn income while preserving their lands.

Shirley Chisholm

1924–2005

Photo courtesy of Wikimedia Commons

Shirley Chisholm was a powerful, intelligent, and empowering woman. She was an American politician, educator, and author. Chisholm became the first African American congresswoman in 1968. Just a few years later, Chisholm became the first major-party black candidate to ever make a bid for the United States presidency.

Charles Hamilton Houston

1895–1950

Photo courtesy of Washington Area Spark/Flickr

Charles Hamilton Houston was a lawyer who played a key role in dismantling the Jim Crow laws and training lawyers like future Supreme Court Justice Thurgood Marshall. He was the first African American to serve as an editor of the *Harvard Law Review,* he fought to put an end to segregation in schools, and he was posthumously awarded the NAACP's Spingarn Medal in 1950.

Ella Baker

1903–1986

Photo courtesy of Library of Congress

Ella Baker committed her life's work to advancing civil rights. She served as the field secretary and national director of branches for the National Association for the Advancement of Colored People (NAACP). Baker helped recruit new members and expand the organization's reach across the United States. Baker served as the executive director of the Southern Christian Leadership Conference (SCLC), a faith-based coalition that applies the principles of nonviolent action to advance social justice. She supported the work of youth leaders with the formation of the Student Nonviolent Coordinating Committee (SNCC). Baker was fondly known as "fundi," a Swahili term for one who shares wisdom and knowledge with the next generation.

DR. ARTIKA TYNER (a.k.a. Miss Freedom Fighter, Esquire) is a passionate educator, an award-winning author, a civil rights attorney, a sought-after speaker, and an advocate for justice who is committed to helping children discover their leadership potential and serve as change agents in the global community. She is the founder of the Planting People Growing Justice Leadership Institute.

JACKLYN MILTON is a lifelong educator and community advocate. She served as a home childcare provider and an early childhood specialist for more than three decades. She is a licensed family life educator who helps families create pathways to success.

About Planting People Growing Justice Leadership Institute

Planting People Growing Justice Leadership Institute seeks to plant seeds of social change through education, training, and community outreach.

All proceeds from the book will be used to support the educational programming of Planting People Growing Justice Leadership Institute.

Learn more at www.ppgjli.org